# RAISED BED GARDENING

A Complete Guide To Build Your
Own Raised Bed Gardening Even
As A Beginner

**ERNEST GREEN**

# Table of Contents

# CHAPTER ONE

# INTRODUCTION

Raised bed gardening manner growing plants in soil that is better than the ground. Maximum usually, you can do this with some form of enclosure or body product of wooden, stone, or maybe bales of hay or repurposed fabric like old dressers.

Raised beds can be as humble or creative as you like. A raised bed planter may be a permanent fixture for perennial vegetation to settle in and mature. The initial price of getting your raised bed set up will rely on how difficult you're making it, but once in area, raised beds are no pricier to hold than conventional gardens. They provide a variety of blessings.

When creating a raised bed instead of moving into-ground, you may place it wherein the solar or color is the quality for the plants you want to domesticate. You could additionally prevent tunneling pests from decimating your plant life. Vegetation may be healthier and extra effective in a raised mattress due to the fact you may manipulate the quality of the soil and water drainage. In case you build the sides wide enough to make a bench, you could even sit down and lawn. For people with returned troubles, that makes it less difficult to tend the flora.

# CHAPTER TWO

# HOW TO CONSTRUCT A SIMPLE RAISED BED GARDENING

There are a whole lot of reasons to build raised vegetable gardens — the type that sit above ground inside a body fabricated from wood or other fabric. If your land has sandy, claylike, or hard-packed soil (or in case you don't understand and don't deliver a hoot about the distinction), you may offer best conditions for something you're keen on developing.

vegetation are lifted out of the way of rowdy pets and babies, and your soil warms up in advance and remains that way longer, extending the growing season and presenting gentler conditions for brand new seeds and delicate transplants. Fruits, greens, and ornamentals will send their roots deeper on the lookout for water, because of this a more potent foundation and stepped forward health. And raised beds preserve your space tidy. First-class of all, they couldn't be less complicated to make. Especially if you're stepping into developing for the primary time, you're going to need some beds of your own.

What you'll want

For a 4-by way of-8-foot bed, you'll want:

• 2 2-by way of-12 planks, every 8 feet lengthy

• 2 2-by using-12 planks, each 4 feet long

• 12 pieces of rebar, each 2 ft lengthy

• A rubber mallet

• Newspaper or cardboard

• Soil to fill the finished frame

1. Position your forums.

On a level section of floor, lay the forums down with their internal corners touching. Stand one long board on its side, and, using a rubber mallet, hammer pieces of rebar 1 foot from every nook, some inches deep into the floor.

2. Prop up the quick aspects. Use a bit of rebar at the middle of each for brief assist. Next, prop up the second long side and modify the alignment of your body as necessary. Then hammer rebar a few inches deep 1 foot from each nook of the second lengthy facet.

3. Add more support.

Hammer rebar some inches deep a foot from each corner of the fast facets and cast off the brief helps. Upload 2 portions of rebar 2 toes apart alongside every long side. Those will reinforce the frame while it's packed with soil. Then hammer in the rebar until 6 to 10 inches are uncovered above ground.

4. Fill it up.

Line the bottom of your frame with newspaper or cardboard and wet it thoroughly. Ultimately, fill your bed with soil to within some inches of the top.

# CHAPTER THREE

# MATERIALS NEEDED IN BUILDING A RAISED BED GARDENING

Here are some materials needed in building your raised bed gardening:

Wattle

Weave a frame with long, flexible sticks. The children may have a laugh accumulating them, and the consequences are commonly Interest-worthy.

Logs

If you've currently cleared a tree, logs can be a cost-effective material. Pick portions which might be instantly and at the least 1 foot in diameter.

Concrete Blocks

Placing the blocks with open ends up gives extra growing room. Tuck herbs or decorative flowers into the cavities.

High and powerful

A waist-high bed is obtainable to those with physical boundaries.

Area

Build your beds someplace that gets at the least 5 to 6 hours of day by day sunlight — the greater, the higher! Orient them north to south to save you plants from shading each other out. Beds need to be at the least a foot wide, even though no greater than 4 feet throughout to make weeding and harvesting workable. 6 to 8 feet lengthy is typical and price-effective, 10 to 14 inches is a great height to house robust roots. Depart as minimum 2 or 3 toes among beds for strolling and wheelbarrow get entry to.

Wooden

The brilliance of a plank-and-rebar layout is that every individual wall is without problems replaced. Strive naturally rot-resistant types of wooden, consisting of oak, cedar, and redwood.

Soil

You want the type that's darkish, wealthy, and loaded with microorganisms. Fill your beds with a combination of 50 to 60% excellent-best topsoil and forty to 50% nicely-elderly compost. Before each new growing season, test your soil for pH and nutrient content. You could purchase a kit at maximum home-development stores. In case your take a look at shows a need for added vitamins like nitrogen and potassium, enhance ranges with the aid of working in amendments along with bone meal and kelp. Dress beds with an additional ½ inch of compost later inside the developing season to boom organic count number and raise soil health.

Plants

In case you're building your beds in excessive summer, it's no longer too overdue to plant fall vegetation. Sow seeds like carrots and lettuce at once into the soil, or buy midseason transplants for crops like kale and broccoli. If you'd alternatively wait till subsequent year to plant, cover the soil in your new raised beds with a combination of grass clippings and shredded leaves in autumn — the fabric will compost earlier than you're prepared to begin in spring.

Water

Raised beds have outstanding drainage, that is brilliant for plant health, but they dry out speedy. Deliver your flowers an extended drink inside the early nighttime, however check them once more on hot summer season afternoons. If the soil is dry, it's a real scorcher outside, or you stay in a hot and arid climate, water again. A programmable drip-irrigation system is less expensive and convenient, delivering regular moisture straight to plant roots. Invest in a timer issue to store cash and water.

# CHAPTER FOUR

# ADVANTAGES OF RAISED BED GARDENING

Raised beds have many advantages. Right here are some reasons why you should have one:

• Garden chores are made less complicated and greater relaxed way to much less bending and kneeling. Shop your knees and returned from the pressure and pain of tending the garden!

• Productiveness of plant life is stepped forward because of higher drainage and deeper rooting.

•	Raised beds are ideal for small spaces in which a traditional row lawn is probably too wild and unwieldy. Raised beds help to keep things prepared and in test.

•	Planting in a raised bed offers you full manipulate over soil exceptional and content material, that is especially critical in areas in which the prevailing soil is rocky, nutrient-terrible, or riddled with weeds.

•	Raised beds allow for an extended developing season, considering that you could work the soil greater quick inside the spring in frost-hardened regions, or convert the bed into a cold frame in the fall.

•	Fewer weeds are seen in raised beds way to the mattress being accelerated far from surrounding weeds and being full of disease- and weed-unfastened soil.

•	Raised beds allow for easier rectangular-foot gardening and companion planting.

# CHAPTER FIVE

# SIZE OF A RAISED BED GARDENING

- First, you want vicinity that has stage floor and receives the right amount of daylight (6 to 8t hours per day). This must slim down your alternatives a bit.

- In terms of bed length, 4 ft is a common width. Lumber is often cut in 4-foot increments, and you additionally need on the way to get admission to the garden without entering into the bed. Making the bed too wide will make it tough to attain the center, which makes weeding and harvesting an ache.

•	Length isn't as critical. Traditional plots are often four toes huge through 8 ft long or 4 feet huge by 12 ft lengthy. Make your mattress so long as you want or build multiple raised beds for exceptional vegetation.

•	The depth of the bed can range, however 6 inches of soil ought to be the minimal. Most garden flora want at least 6 to 12 inches for their roots, so 12 inches is ideal.

## *Preparing your site*

•      Earlier than you set up the bed, break up and unfasten the soil below with a garden fork in order that it's no longer compacted. Cross about 6 to 8 inches deep. For stepped forward rooting, a few gardeners like to cast off the pinnacle layer (about a spade's depth), dig down every other layer, and then go back the pinnacle layer and mix the soil layers collectively.

•      in case you're planning to position your raised mattress in a area currently occupied by using a lawn, lay down a sheet of cardboard, a tarp, or a chunk of landscaping fabric to kill off the grass first. After about 6 weeks (or less, relying on the weather), the grass should be lifeless and will be a lot less complicated to remove.

•	To help wooden beds, vicinity wooden stakes at each nook (and each few feet for longer beds). Location at the inside of the bed in order that the stakes are less seen.

•	power the stakes about 60% (2 feet) into the ground and go away the rest of the stakes uncovered aboveground.

- make sure that the stakes are level in order that they're inside the ground on the equal height, otherwise you'll have uneven beds.

- Set the lowest forums a pair inches underground stage. Take a look at that they are stage.

- Use galvanized nails (or screws) to restore the forums to the stakes.

- add any extra rows of forums, solving them to the stakes, too.

### *Soil for Raised lawn Beds*

The soil combo which you positioned into your raised mattress is its maximum vital aspect. Greater gardens fail or falter due to bad soil than nearly anything else.

•      Fill the beds with a mixture of topsoil, compost, and other organic material, which includes manure, to offer your plant life nutrient-rich surroundings (see recipes underneath). Study greater approximately soil amendments and making ready soil for planting.

- Observe that the soil in a raised bed will dry out extra speedy. In the course of the spring and fall, this is fine, however for the duration of the summer time, add straw, mulch, or hay on top of the soil to help it keep moisture.

- Common watering can be critical with raised beds, specifically within the early tiers of plant increase. In any other case, raised beds want little upkeep.

When the use of flexible fabric along with lumber, the strain of the soil will reason the wooden to bow out. You have to offer staking halfway down the period and comfortable the timber to it to save you this outward bowing.

If using timber, build the body so that the wooden grain on all forums is facing inward. Otherwise, they may shy away and curve towards the outdoor as the wood dries and weathers. Not simplest is this ugly, however it may additionally pull the screws or nails out as properly, making your beds much less secure.

Speak me of screws, I prefer them as opposed to nails for securing the timber. Screws are forgiving in case you make a mistake. But be sure to apply all-climate timber screws with a duration of at least 3 inches. To prevent splitting, it is a superb concept to drill pilot holes first, specifically closer to the ends of each piece.

Premade kits are now effectively available that encompass connecting joints and hinges so that you can configure your bed form and height pretty much anyway you'd like. Those devices make mattress setup a snap, and no production is needed. With regards to simplicity for raised-mattress construction, those kits are best. You could find them via many catalog and mail-order lawn-supply organizations.

If you really want to have a lovely and effective garden, give raised beds a try.

THE END